MARY AUDREY RAYCROFT

ONCE UPON A REVIVAL

A *subjective look* at the Toronto revival

FOREWORD BY BARBARA J. YODER

DEDICATION

This book is dedicated to all those who venture out to "follow the cloud" of the Holy Spirit into unchartered territory and embrace an ongoing amazing adventure of faith

ACKNOWLEDGEMENTS

Thank you, Holy Spirit, for giving me a good memory! Thank you for leading me in choosing which of the countless events to share; knowing what would be appropriate for this book and what to set aside for another time.

Thank you to the many encouragers who, over the past two years, have urged, prodded and bugged me to "write the book". Not even realizing what it would be about, you just "saw it" and knew that a book had to be written. "You have a story to tell" many repeated.

Thank you, Sue Richards and Faith Marie Baczko. I am extremely grateful for you both. You were incredibly helpful in editing the final product and preparing the manuscript for production. Thank you Benjamin Deitrick for designing such a great cover!

ENDORSEMENTS

Few people are as suited as Mary Audrey Raycroft to write reflections about the Toronto Outpouring. She was in it from the beginning, and was an eye witness and participant of that first night of January 20, 1994. This is an amazing story and happened as she tells it. But be careful, the Holy Spirit is mightily on these pages.

John and Carol Arnott
Founding Pastors, Catch the Fire, Toronto

As someone who has been part of Catch the Fire since 1994, this book made me smile. As I read Mary Audrey's reflections, heard her stories, and pondered her insights, I was taken back to many of my own memories of how God came to our church. This is a great overview of what happened, how it happened and how to keep revival fires flowing in our lives.

Steve Long
Senior Leader, Catch the Fire Toronto

Every testimony is pregnant with seeds of hundreds more like it. Mary Audrey's eyewitness account of the habitation God made for himself in Toronto is a valuable and inspiring piece of revival inheritance for each of us to possess. Her real time experiences and observations of the real people whose ordinary lives are forever altered by a REAL GOD should be eaten like a feast and drunk like the best libation to cross the lips of your soul! In a generation grappling with shifting global culture, economic uncertainty, and an increasing flood of information, *"Once Upon a Revival..."* is an insider's handbook for what the world needs now: encounter with our Father.

The river of His presence that opened and poured into and through the lives of the stewards of revival at Airport church is still flowing and still free. Every person, pastor, professor and professional, optimist, skeptic, pessimist and parent, should step under the spout offered us through *"Once Upon a Revival..."* We have the tremendous honor of coming to know Mary Audrey in the early days of the outpouring. Her sagely wisdom and childlike heart of devotion to Jesus together with her mountain moving faith make Mary Audrey a unique kingdom treasure.

Though she would never think of it, lovers of the Presence owe a debt of gratitude to this astonishing laid down lover of God. May you be carried away on God's river as you journey with her in *"Once Upon a Revival..."* and re-encounter one of the most sweeping moves of God in our lifetime thus far.

Mahesh and Bonnie Chavda,
Founders of the Watch of the Lord,
All Nations Church, Charlotte, North Carolina USA

The Holy Spirit's outpouring on our church in 1994 changed our lives forever! We have so enjoyed working alongside Mary Audrey for these past 20 years as Associate Pastors together in this renewal. Her love for the Holy Spirit is so evident! You are sure to marvel over God's continual blessings and enjoy the humor as you read Mary Audrey's down-to-earth renditions from her unique perspective.

Connie & Jeremy Sinnott
Associate Pastors/Worship Leaders/
International Trainers, Catch the Fire Toronto

CONTENTS

PREFACE

"Tell me a story" is an age-old request from both the old and the young and so often the response begins with "Once upon a time ..."

Recently, many leaders and believers from a variety of denominations and streams have been questioning me about what happened in 1994 when the Holy Spirit burst forth upon our small Vineyard church in the city of Mississauga, a community touching the western suburbs of Toronto, Ontario, Canada: questions such as "What was it like?"; "What did you experience?"; "What happened?"; "What did you see?"; "How did you handle all of 'that'?" "Please tell us the story."

This book, *"Once Upon a Revival..."* is in response to those who ask, with the hope that I can paint a picture of one of the most revitalizing, renewing, refreshing, challenging, controversial, on-going moves of the Holy Spirit in recent history. Furthermore, I'd like to shed light on some issues for sceptics who read it and bring clarity and understanding where there has been ignorance, false impressions, and criticism.

Be aware that what I have written in *"Once Upon a Revival ..."* is from a purely subjective viewpoint. In other words, it is not a theological paper or a doctrinally correct thesis, but simply my observations and experiences that I have lived with over the past two decades.

An old television detective series had as its introduction, "There are a million stories in the naked city. This is just one of them." So there must be thousands of stories (perhaps millions) which could be told about "The Toronto Blessing", as it became known. This is just one of them.

What you read is just one small side of a multi-faceted gem designed by God to draw to the world's attention that His Kingdom is very much alive and well and manifesting on planet earth.

Mary Audrey Raycroft, September 2013

FOREWORD

Barbara J. Yoder

I am a revival junkie. I always have been. My passion for revival has only grown exponentially over the years. I am a product of a revival; was groomed by a revivalist; and am desperate for revival, ongoing revival. Revival is life, a vital living, loving, overcoming relationship with Jesus through the Holy Spirit which constantly transforms and ignites us.

It is the explosion of God's life giving Spirit among us. (1 Cor. 15:45) Revival is a release of God's presence in an unusual and enormous dimension transforming us from deadness into a living vibrancy. It creates a heart on fire for God. Resultantly, His life, His agenda, and His mandate for us become uppermost in our heart and mind. He captures us and hijacks our life for His purpose and glory.

Revival to me is what part of the core of the New Testament Church was about. It is what happened to the 120 in the Upper Room. They went from confused, depressed, hope deferred followers of Jesus to revived, consumed and fiery lovers of Him. That meeting place with the Holy Spirit propelled them into the midst of the city's marketplace where they immediately infected those present and 3000 people instantly were added to the church. They went from 120 to 3,120 because 120 people were overcome and propelled with new power, excitement and love into the midst of the marketplace to affect others. They did not go out of duty but out of being overcome by the Holy Spirit. The Church in that day moved forward into territory after territory ignited by and igniting others with the power of the Word and the Holy Spirit. How? Through a revived, renewed, overcoming relationship with Jesus.

Three to four years ago, struggling with confusion over my God-given identity, I finally stumbled onto the fact that first and foremost I am a revivalist. It was then that I simultaneously was introduced to and became friends with Mary Audrey Raycroft. In fact when the prophetic word clearly came forth as to my new identity, Mary Audrey was with me and laid hands on me with others. I desperately wanted everything she possessed and experienced. I was drawn to that sense of ongoing revival, the overcoming life-giving presence of God she constantly carried whether she realized it or not. I didn't want her to remove her hands from me until I knew that what she carried had been imparted to me. I wanted what she had.

That passion for Jesus, for an ongoing love infested, living, vital, vibrating, transforming, infecting, overcoming relationship with Him consumed me. It actually had been there for years but was now being highlighted because it was time for something new. It was time for me to pioneer a whole new way for followers of Jesus in my sphere of influence. And it was Mary Audrey that God brought into my life to help me get there. I would sit with her for hours asking her questions, mining everything I could from her treasure filled chest of revival experience at Toronto .

I knew I was to be instrumental in igniting revival so everything she knew and possessed I longed to know and experience. How did the revival start? What happened to John and Carol Arnott that propelled Toronto Airport Christian Fellowship into revival? What part did Randy Clark play? What were the highlights of the revival? How did they prepare all the people needed to help with what was happening? What about some of the seemingly controversial things people talked about? How did the revival change the people? What were some of the funny stories? How did it manifest in all of its varied ways? How did they handle quirky or difficult people? How was I to prepare for revival? What did I need to know ahead of time to avoid unnecessary problems or challenges? On and on the questions went. And to this day, I refuse to leave her alone. When a new question comes up I bug her until I get an answer.

This is a woman who gave up her "regular life" for 20 years to nurture, train, equip people to minister to those coming to TACF, now Catch The Fire, revival meetings. In fact my husband and I sat under her teaching in the pastor's meetings at TACF within a year after the revival started. She was part of the core team that fueled the ongoing revival through equipping and training people to minister in the midst of revival day and night. Her life as it had been, was suddenly taken from her and consumed by this revival that broke out in 1994 and never ended. A revival that though it has morphed into many nations, is still ongoing in Toronto, Canada.

I never dreamed Mary Audrey would become part of my life. I never dreamed she would help fuel the passion in my heart to see not only individual revival but the fire of revival break out in the midst of the church. I never dreamed she would become a dear friend and colleague sharing my all consuming and desperate passion for God's presence.

I love this book. This book is Mary Audrey. It is her story of what she has eaten, breathed, slept, drank, lived out in the last 20 years. It is the nitty gritty story of what she discovered, uncovered and stumbled upon while living in the midst of and teaching the ministry teams in ongoing revival. Glean everything you can from this book. It is truth and it is life, the story of how Jesus revealed Himself in both profound and utterly hysterical ways. It is a manual as well, helping us know how to think, pray and act when revival breaks out. Most of all, it is the story of one woman, impacted deeply by revival who has now become a carrier of revival as well as a preparer of the way for revival.

This book is a treasure to me. I believe it will be so to you as well. Read it from cover to cover and treasure it, hold it close to you. You are going to need all the treasures of knowledge and experience Mary Audrey shared because we are on the verge of a fresh outpouring of the Holy Spirit which will bring revival to the church and awakening to the world.

Barbara J. Yoder, Founder and Apostolic Overseer, Shekinah Regional Apostolic Center, Ann Arbor, Michigan:

Author of The Breaker Anointing, Taking On Goliath, The Overcomer's Anointing, God's Bold Call To Women and The Cry God Hears

INTRODUCTION

Let me begin this story by emphasizing the core values of Catch The Fire church in Toronto (once known as Toronto Airport Vineyard and then Toronto Airport Christian Fellowship). Such values have not diminished over the years, but have grown in depth of understanding and are the basis for its whole ministry. These have been the foundation stones from the beginning, even before the revival began in 1994.

I place these before you so you can understand what keeps our church community anchored. They are possibly one of the key factors in our being able to nurture a revival culture over the past twenty years.

We have come to embrace the acrostic for the word fire - F.I.R.E. – to describe these anchoring values.

F. Father:

We value knowing God as Father as a relationship with the Him is everything! Experiencing God as our true Father, just like Jesus did, will change our lives. Every child of

God needs to feel, know, and experience the unconditional, extravagant love of Father God, so knowing His heart is an essential foundational stone.

I. Intimacy with God:

We value hearing His voice; developing a passion, for Jesus; learning to love Him and His Presence both personally and corporately.

R. Renewing the Heart:

We value getting healed from the wounds of life. We are well aware that wounded, intimidated, controlled, abused people - yes, even Christians and even Christian leaders - wound, intimidate, control and abuse others. All of us in leadership at Catch The Fire go through a Healing Week with Restoring The Foundations Ministry.

Before we can truly love others, we must love ourselves and that means allowing the Spirit of God to transform our spirits and souls. Our Father is able to reveal to us issues and hurts that need healing. The Holy Spirit knows what we need to believe and receive in order to become whole ourselves so that our ministry to others flows from a pure heart.

E. Equipping and Empowering the Body of Christ.

> We believe in teaching and equipping every believer, releasing them with the tools necessary to minister to others.[1]

These core values are the underlying principles that guide us in ministering to people, making decisions, determining priorities, setting goals, allocating resources, and carrying out programs. They are the defining characteristics of Catch The Fire and a vital part of nurturing the revival culture that's there, known as the Toronto Blessing.

It has been a privilege to be part of Catch The Fire's team since before the revival began; to partake and be a witness of an incredible move of God in our midst. May those who read this be able to capture some of the wonder we experienced as we chose to welcome the Holy Spirit into our church.

---

[1] Ephesians 4: 11,12

Chapter One

THE WAY WE WERE

B
efore January 20, 1994 we were a nice, comfortable, equipping church with about 200 people in the fellowship. A strong emphasis was placed on growing in an understanding of and embracing the reality of God as a very personal, compassionate Father and, as His children, allowing Him to heal us of life's hurts. We had been linked with the Vineyard movement for several years and highly valued the indwelling and empowering Holy Spirit, training those in the fellowship to minister to others. There was a team of about 30 mature believers who were able to assist in altar ministry and pray in depth with people as needed. With a smile now, I can say we thought we were just fine as a church: normal, respectable, not boring, friendly, and definitely not controversial or one that "rocked a lot of boats".

Located in a two-room end unit of a small strip mall, right at the end of the airport runway where the massive 747s took off, we had become accustomed to the shaking and rumbling and noise of those massive jet engines as they accelerated overhead.

Our senior pastor, John Arnott, had such a longing to see healing manifested in the church's ministry. He believed that there was so much more to walking in the Kingdom than he and his wife Carol were experiencing, both personally and as a church family.

They each began to really press in to God, seriously seeking the Lord's face and His heart. They turned their mornings over to Jesus for many months, staying home from the office, quietly worshipping Jesus and immersing themselves in the Word. Those of you who know Pastor John will have a hard time seeing this highly motivated visionary, entrepreneurial leader, who always has had the latest piece of communications technology almost grafted on to him, turning off his phone and computer. These were the times before IPhone, IPad, Skype, Facebook, Texting and all the electronic gadgets we have nowadays, but whatever was current then, he had it with him every moment and was always "turned on". Those were the good old days when he actually had time to enjoy flying his model airplanes with buddies in a farmer's field. Now everything was set aside for those intimate mornings with the Lord. Hunger for God far surpassed anything else.

Along with the growing hunger for God, I believe there were several factors which the Spirit engineered in preparing the Arnotts' hearts for the revival that lay ahead. Firstly, in the year prior to the giving of their mornings to Jesus, while in South America, they received a strong prophetic blessing from Claudio Friedzon which spoke of new life in the Spirit which would be powerfully released within and from them. Secondly, they became aware of the revival identified by joy and laughter happening through the ministry of Rodney Howard-Brown, although had never actually attended any of his meetings. Thirdly, they connected with a fellow Vineyard minister and friend Randy Clark from St. Louis who had recently returned from a life-changing encounter with the Holy Spirit at a Rodney Howard-Brown revival meeting in Tulsa. The testimony was that Randy's church in St. Louis was incredibly "set on fire" and deeply impacted by the Lord after their pastor returned home with a noticeably fresh anointing. Randy's gentle enthusiasm was contagious and John Arnott, always with an adventurous spirit and wanting everything God would give to his church family, invited Randy to Toronto to bring any blessing he'd received to our local church near the airport.

And thus began the story, which is now history.

Chapter Two

A New Beginning

On a cold winter's night, Thursday, January 20, 1994 about 120 people gathered in the sanctuary for an unusual evening meeting - unusual in that we seldom had mid-week meetings, especially on a Thursday, unless they were part of one of our yearly conferences. Randy Clark, a Vineyard pastor from St. Louis had been invited to share his recent experiences with the Holy Spirit in a revival context and to pray for our church family if led to do so. He planned on being with us for four evenings, ending with a healing meeting on the Sunday with John Arnott.

The facility had two meeting areas, one being the sanctuary with about 197 moveable chairs, a smallish angled platform for the worship team in one corner, and a tiny sound booth up near the ceiling which the technicians had to reach by a ladder fastened to the wall. The other room next door, around the same size, was used for the Sunday School, various equipping programs and the odd church supper. It also held about 197 chairs if needed. It had exit doors to the parking lot so people could leave without having to pass through the sanctuary. There also was one small bathroom, a tiny office area, a room for the pastor and a storage room. Finally, believe it or not, there was a small café from which we could serve coffee and hot dogs – a precursor I guess for the very professional cafeteria we now operate years later. We had two pastoral leaders, John Arnott and Jeremy Sinnott who was also the leader of our small worship team, plus one half-time secretary. I share these little details with you so you can appreciate the setting we were working in when God broke into our lives

SURPRISED BY THE HOLY SPIRIT

That memorable evening I was teaching a class on the Motivational Gifts in this other room. When it was dismissed around 10:00 p.m. and the students had left the building, I decided to slip across the hall and through a side entrance into the sanctuary to see what was going on. I'd heard worship music earlier but now everything seemed strangely quiet and yet I knew people were in there because the parking lot was still full.

Then came the surprise and the beginning of countless blessings and interactions with the Holy Spirit. When I opened the door to the sanctuary the most amazing thing happened. With a mighty "whoosh" a wind blew through the doorway, knocking me off of my feet laying me flat on my back and simultaneously my face became numb from my chin up to my lower eyelids. Then my lips and face began to tingle with a sensation similar to that which happens when dental freezing is coming out. I was unable to make a sound for about 20 minutes. Later, some friends jokingly said the Lord was shutting me up from talking so much while other kinder types said it must have been an anointing for future verbal ministry. Whatever happened, my life was forever changed!

When finally able to move, I crawled on my hands and knees through the doorway and looking into the room could see no one on their chairs; they were on the floor under and beside them and sounds of laughter were beginning around the room. I remember our pastors standing on the far side of the room looking with amazement at the scene. The worship team members were flat on the floor with several having fallen off the back of the small stage. To this day, I wonder what happened to those people in the ceiling high sound booth.

Was this simply a one-night phenomena or would there be more?

Chapter Three

CHANGED BEYOND MEASURE!

All heaven broke loose, not just that night, but night after night for weeks and then months. The kabod, the weighty presence of the Spirit, was tangible each night as the Lord poured out immense refreshing, joy, healing, and restoration. I remember, almost shyly, fearful of presumption, using the word "revival" in conversations. Renewal, refreshing, restoration seemed safer. Probably that was because what happened did not seem to compare to any other "revival" I'd ever heard of or read about.

Our whole church structure and programs were drastically altered. As the word got around that something amazing was happening in that little church at the end of the runway, people from many different places began to arrive. Our own church family began to feel quite displaced as by that first summer there were close to 1200 people crammed into those two rooms. How we ever managed to be missed by the fire department and closed down is a mystery to me. Crowds lined up on the sidewalk surrounding the building beginning around 2:00 p.m. each afternoon, winter and summer. Some brought their lawn chairs, barbecues and coolers. There was simply no place to park so many cars and we finally rented a field about ½ a mile away. The people, including our senior leaders, now had a long walk. We even became organized enough to hand out numbered tickets based on the amount of chairs we could cram into the building plus standing room space.

Not only arriving hours ahead of the services, the people simply did not want to go home either. Night after night, immersed in the Lord's presence, many would stay until 2:00 or 3:00 a.m. even though they had to go to work just a few hours later. We would carry people out in the wee hours of the morning and deposit them on the grass outside just so we could turn the lights off and go home ourselves.

I remember two ushers rolling out, on a furniture dolly, a certain stately, white-haired Supreme Court judge and unceremoniously dumping him on a grassy knoll. East Indian turbaned cab drivers would line up to take people home or to their hotels. At times we would assign designated drivers for those who became so lost (drunk) in the Spirit that they couldn't drive themselves. There are testimonies from those who were actually able to handle their cars but were pulled over by the police because of their erratic driving. Breathalyser tests proved there was no alcohol involved.

NO LONGER "COMFORTABLE"

Everything we considered as proper church protocol changed drastically. It's as if God was determined to shake all the religious starch and tradition out of us so He could fashion us into being a people who would carry His Presence, not only to our community but to the world. I felt He said, "I've given you (the church) 2000 years to get your act together and be my people of testimony and now I will show you how to be My church, My way! It's time for a shift – some things will change."

The Spirit came like a giant tsunami tidal wave which swept over and changed everything in its path. He got our attention first in unprecedented ways which shook us to the core of our being. Those tsunamis stir up and clear out a lot of debris and over time we found that much personal debris was being revealed and washed out of each of us.

I remember one prophetic word which said, "God will often offend your mind to reveal what's in your heart." Yuk, I didn't like that! For years I had taught people the adage, "The Holy Spirit's a

35

gentleman; He'll never offend." Ha, where did that ever come from! It fits into the category of those "Christianese" sayings such as "God helps those who help themselves", or "Cleanliness is next to Godliness" or "God gave you a mind and expects you to use it". I owe apologies to many people for having given that impression over the years prior to 1994. The Holy Spirit will definitely offend our religious mindsets whenever necessary, especially when they stand in His way.

NO MORE CONVENTIONAL BEHAVIOUR

In a later chapter there are stories of how people responded to the Spirit's presence but for now I need to describe some of those beginning days. Laughter was a main ingredient of the nightly meetings ... without provocation, with nothing specifically funny happening, it would burst out - especially through the quiet, slightly stuffy Christians. Joy became one of the by-products of the revival. Actually, the laughter manifestation has remained to some extent throughout the years and we have seen a fulfillment of Proverbs 17:22, "a merry heart does good like medicine", as healing has occurred within people's bodies following times of this Holy Spirit rib-tickling laughter.

Our half- time church secretary, Donna, was really impacted by the "tsunami" - so much so that she could only speak in tongues when answering the phone. You can imagine that this created quite a problem when the phone began to ring off the wall. We had to hire extra office help just to handle the phone. One day Donna answered a call from New Zealand and instead of "Good morning, Toronto Airport Vineyard" she broke into tongues. At that very moment the anointing of the Spirit whizzed through the phone lines, knocking the pastor who was calling off of his feet and right through into his office staff, who fell to the floor as well. Who can explain this????

Along with the laughter, many peoples' arms, legs and bodies would begin shaking vigorously as they lay on the floor under the power of the Spirit. One rather sophisticated, handsome Texas pastor shook so hard that he literally shot off his cowboy boots catapulting them across the room. Those kinds of boots usually can only be removed with a boot-jack. Others would be "frozen" as if paralyzed or stuck in one spot when they went to the pulpit area to preach or give testimony. Others would be struck dumb when they tried to speak or could only express themselves with halting stutters.

Having come from a charismatic but still conservative background I had been taught that all this hand and arm shaking in meetings was just caused by either too much "spiritual excitement"; the need to look spiritual in front of others; or an established religious/denominational pattern. "One could stop it at any time", I thought. Before 1994 I used to say to people, "Why are you doing this? It's annoying, you know, please don't do that".

While I believe that some people do get carried away with their emotions and express unusual or disruptive behaviour, what was happening during this outpouring of the Spirit was quite different. Learning to adapt was a challenge. I came to understand that, for many, shaking is simply the result of the body responding to the Holy Spirit's presence or touch. As we are all "wired" differently, we all will respond differently to the Spirit's power. Obviously and thankfully there are no clones in the Kingdom.

Holding the convictions I explained in the last paragraph, I for years had taught against those things. Now everything I had taught against was happening not only around me but right in front of me. My concept of proper church behaviour was totally ruined and I became a "guilty participant" as well.

New loud sounds and exuberant verbal expressions began to be heard even during the preaching. One of the first such sounds, like that of a roaring lion, came forth from a visiting very prestigious, well-established Chinese pastor from western Canada. Everyone's hair stood on end! Once the fierce roaring ceased, he then loudly proclaimed, "The Lion of the tribe of Judah will overcome the dragon of the Orient." It's worth noting that now, twenty years later, there are reports of at least thirty-thousand salvations happening daily all over China as multitudes of people are meeting their Lion, Jesus.

People were falling to the floor, spontaneously touched by the Spirit's power, not simply during prayer ministry times but during the meeting as well. The floor was covered with bodies; we couldn't wear skirts anymore because we had to step over people's faces all the time. It was as if when the Spirit decided to move on a person in this fashion He would do it – period! The Vineyard model at that time was to make people stay standing when receiving prayer. Ministry helpers would literally prop them up so they wouldn't fall over while being ministered to. Well, the Spirit displayed a sense of humour when He would simply have someone collapse to the floor straight down.

WANTING GOD MORE THAN PROTOCOL

The church pastors and leaders were challenged beyond any past experience in knowing how to handle all of this. Six years previously, in John Arnott's Stratford, Ontario church, Jubilee Vineyard, there began a similar breakout of "revival" activity. However it was so unusual and unfamiliar that John shut it down with the attitude, "we don't want any of 'that' in here!" It simply was not in his agenda or the mandate of the church. Also, it was in a season before his intense growing hunger for God, the prophetic encounter with Claudio Friedzon, hearing about Rodney Howard-Brown, and interacting with Randy Clark.

Now, in 1994, as the Spirit burst forth at the little Toronto Vineyard church, our pastor, John, heard a very straightforward, strong admonition from God, "This is My work! Keep your hands off it." John took that very seriously and desperately wanting the Lord's Presence more than anything else, to the best of his ability, he released the controls to his heavenly Father. We found ourselves in a giant "learning curve".

Night after night, John would begin the evening meeting by asking the people, in advance, to forgive us for bringing correction and shutting things down when it was actually the Holy Spirit at work and, alternatively, for not shutting things down when it was an over-dose of the flesh or even the enemy. We did not have a "grid" for any of this. We only knew that we wanted God more than anything else and were willing to let things flow as we were learning to discern Him in the midst of it all.

Once when a concerned visitor cornered John with the accusation that what was happening with some individuals was demonic, his response was, "Wow, are they going in or coming out? That's the question." The need for appropriating the supernatural gift of Discerning of Spirits (1Cor.12:10) became paramount.

Were the manifestations those of the Holy Spirit, a person's own natural spirit and emotions, or of the enemy? They can all look or sound alike and without such discerning, one can make wrong assumptions based solely on human reasoning, personal likes and dislikes, familiar comfort zones, or denominational biases.

THE HUNGRY AND THIRSTY ARRIVED

Pastors and leaders from all denominations began to come from literally all over the world – for the most part they were tired and discouraged, many ready to leave the ministry. The Holy Spirit drew them to a place of refreshing, restoration and new hope. They came from the nations and most importantly met Father God who loved them and moved deeply into their hearts.

We became known as a "River" church, one where there was a flow of the river of God in obvious, recognizable, and life-changing ways. A number of times in scripture the Holy Spirit is described as being like a river:

*How priceless is your unfailing love, O God! People take refuge in the shadow of your wings. They feast on the abundance of your house; you give them drink from your **river** of delights. For with you is the fountain of life; in your light we see light.* Psalms 36:7-9 (NIV)

On the last and greatest day of the festival, Jesus stood and said in a loud voice, "Let anyone who is thirsty

41

come to me and drink.[38] *Whoever believes in me, as Scripture has said, **rivers** of living water will flow from within them." By this he meant the Spirit, whom those who believed in him were later to receive. Up to that time the Spirit had not been given, since Jesus had not yet been glorified.* John 7:37-39 (NIV)

We became a watering hole of refreshing for thousands – many were like dry parched ground, like withered plants, like dried-out old leaves, like hard old sponges. As people began to be immersed in the river of the Spirit they became softened again in their hearts and attitudes – from being stiff and brittle to being pliable and moldable in His hands.

A TIME CONSUMING REVIVAL

None of us wanted to miss a meeting for months!!! "What would the Holy Spirit do next?" we wondered? "Would He be there at all?? Would He always feel welcome?" We had so many questions! We were like little children trying to understand new things.

We held about seventeen meetings every week for the first several years. As well as each evening, there were two meetings during the day primarily for teaching the Word, learning about the Father's heart, training for ministry teams, specific fellowship and interaction with local pastors, and welcoming leaders from the nations. New alignments, cross-denominationally, were being made and fostered.

We finally realized that we needed some "down time" and took Mondays off to breathe and do laundry. Also, we had to make many personal adjustments for the sake of our families, many who felt overwhelmed with the intensity of what was happening at the church, especially with their Moms and Dads.

SQUEEZED OUT OF SPACE

In 1995 as the revival began accelerating even more, we knew our little quarters at the end of the runway could no longer accommodate the crowds and meet our practical needs. A search began for more space and we were introduced to our present facility. Still near the airport, it was a 72,000 square foot building, which had been designed as a commercial trade show center and almost prophetically the address was on Attwell Drive…..at the well! The huge down payment for the purchase poured in from people around the world whose lives had been drastically changed by God's life-giving love. We now could seat around 3,000 people, at last had a large parking lot and much more sidewalk space for the line-ups.

This exciting move of God's Spirit brought costly challenges our way!

Chapter Four

REVIVAL COSTS!

L et me assure you, revival costs! It may cost you money, your reputation, friendships, time, long term commitment, setting other programs aside – and you become famously known as ones who rock religious boats and systems. It's amazing how people want to separate from you when you begin to march to the tune of a different drummer.

Serious choices had to be made. Were we willing to stay in this flow for the long haul? Daily we would wonder if the Holy Spirit would (to put it bluntly) show up. Actually, our only call was to make Him welcome and as John Arnott often said, "We want Him more than anything else in the world. So we'll do whatever is necessary to make room for Him."

A SURGE OF GROWTH

On the practical front, we were literally forced to search for much more ministry and office space to facilitate a quickly enlarging staff and volunteers. We also had begun an exciting five-month School of Ministry, training young adults in leadership skills with prophetic and healing components. The school needed its own building and so a warehouse was purchased a short distance away from the Attwell location.

Within a year we were handling about 4,000 phone calls a week plus a monstrous influx of mail, mostly "snail mail" because e-mail hadn`t yet become a way of life to the extent it is today. Over the next couple of years we grew to about a dozen pastoral leaders plus 120 paid full & part-time staff, plus a security team and volunteer helpers needed just to handle the work load and care for the people.

The Lord's revival presence was not limited to the services in the sanctuary.

Later, as the staff and office teams grew, we had to direct them not to pray for each other during office hours because numerous ones would be touched by the power of God and, falling out of their chairs, they would get stuck under their desks. Some days there would be little work accomplished.

In addition to the night meetings, we began to host large conferences with a variety of themes, about ten a year. We had to make property changes to handle all the traffic and made plans to enlarge our parking lot. Now, we found ourselves in a "catch-22" situation requiring that more money be spent. Because of city by-laws we couldn't put in more parking spaces until we put in more toilets so while renovations were underway for the new bathrooms, people had to park their cars on various factory premises in the neighbourhood. During this interim time, we rented a dozen portable "Johnny-on-the-Spots" and stood them outside, behind the church, for people's convenience during conferences. Then, because so many people were crossing the road after parking their cars all over the place, we had to pay the city $30,000 to put in a cross-walk so people could get safely over the road...and on and on and on! Revival Costs!

OUT OF THE NEST

One costly and painful fact is that revival can bring about a separation in alliances when there's a difference in vision and direction. And so, in the second year of the Spirit's outpouring, the Vineyard head office felt that we needed to go our separate ways, as our mandate and ministry style became so different.

As well, I believe there was concern about the outward manifestations that were happening. Who could logically understand or explain them? Also, a number of Vineyard pastors were being deeply touched in new ways by the Holy Spirit and they wanted to carry this fresh anointing to their own congregations.

Established, identifiable patterns were being rocked. The differing views were quite understandable. However, you may remember that our senior pastor had been directed quite clearly by the Holy Spirit to "keep his hands off!" He was in a very challenging position, trying to balance the call of God with the mandate of his denomination.

The time of separation was painful for us all as we honoured and loved our Vineyard leaders and family of churches. This painful dynamic almost always occurs when something of such magnitude happens – painful for both sides. Painful for the ones who have oversight because they don't understand it and for those who know they can't go back because they feel they have a new mandate. This could be considered rebellion but is actually obedience to a higher authority.

Actually, in hindsight, we could see that it was all in the Lord's plan as this move of the Spirit was to cross over many denominations with an unprecedented outreach around the world. One great benefit was to bring alongside us wonderful men and women - apostles, prophets, evangelists and leaders of integrity and wisdom who have poured into us over the years. They have given us advice, affirmation and suggestions for adjustments where needed. We continue to be thoroughly blessed in these various alignments!

Thankfully, we were supported – I'd like to say "held tightly in love" – by many of these precious new alignments as we learned how to plough through the unusual and uncharted days ahead.

Chapter Five

WHAT ON EARTH IS GOING ON!!

Probably one of the most controversial aspects of the revival in Toronto has been the whole issue of manifestations. You may find that John Arnott's book or CD set, *Manifestations and Prophetic Symbolism* would be of interest and encouragement.

Manifestations and unusual behaviour have been challenges during revivals ever since the day of Pentecost when the disciples were accused of being drunk (Acts 2:13-16). It's so easy to misunderstand and criticize those things that are outside of our comfort zones! Now I am able to laugh at myself as I recall my own personal reactions during those early years of exuberant, noisy, body-shaking joy. I'd love to say, tongue in cheek, that I was never judgemental or critical but was definitely observational – smile. I had to learn to not reject the activity immediately but be willing to watch and wait to see if there was any subsequent good fruit in a person's life as a result of all the "revival activity".

OBSERVING THE UNUSUAL

We are exhorted in 1 Thessalonians 5:19-22 to test (weigh) everything; to not quench (stifle) the Holy Spirit; to not scoff at prophecies but to test everything that is said; to hold on to what is good. I think that can be applied to not just what is said, but also to everything that is acted out. Testing does not quench the Spirit; sin and disunity does. In my opinion, testing clears the path for more of the Spirit to move.

Sometimes comments were made by outside pastors after observing or hearing about the behaviours at the revival meetings. They spoke such pronouncements as, "That's just the flesh manifesting! I definitely don't and won't have any of that sinful flesh stuff in my church!" A protective attitude would rise up in me when I heard this and, while I never openly verbalized it, I wanted to say, "Of course not! There's no flesh ever manifested in your place; never any gossip, back-biting, criticism, selfish ambition, control, immorality, or jealousy."

Granted, I am sure that many, many times what went on was an expression of child-like exuberance and was definitely natural, not supernatural. Yes, it was an expression of the flesh, however I don't see that it could ever be construed as sinful. King David, in Psalm 103:1 commands his soul to bless the Lord with all that is within him. It's as though he is commanding his soul to choose to express praise, "soul, rise up and do it!" Many times he says, "I **will** praise the Lord!"

> *"I **will** be glad and rejoice in you; I **will** sing the praises of your name, O Most High."*

> — Psalm 9:1-3 NIV

> *"…that my heart may sing your praises and not be silent. Lord my God, I **will** praise you forever."*

> — Psalm 30:11-12 NIV

> *"Why, my soul, are you downcast? Why so disturbed within me? Put your hope in God, for I **will** yet praise him, my Savior and my God."*

> — Psalm 42:4-6 NIV

> *"Because your love is better than life, **my lips will** glorify you."*

> — Psalm 63:2-4 NIV

> *"My heart, O God, is steadfast; I **will** sing and make music with all my soul."*

> — Psalm 108:1-3 NIV

I wonder if when he joyfully danced through the streets in Jerusalem stripped down to his "bare essentials", were his actions of the flesh or of the Spirit? Just asking.

As well, there's validity in knowing the person manifesting and thus easier to weigh what's going on. Are they part of the church family or an outsider? Do we know their hearts, their general attitudes and behaviours? As previously mentioned in Chapter Three, we needed the ability to discern the source of the manifestation, either through a supernatural revelation or by knowing the fruit and track record in the life of the person.

OUT OF CHARACTER ACTIVITIES

Picture the scene when a lovely member of our church family - a very gentle, unassuming, discreet, highly proper intercessor walked across the floor in front of the platform crowing like an early morning rooster. There were around 2000 people in the sanctuary that night. During that week we were visited by several major American and Canadian television networks to capture on film what was happening. The revival was catching the attention of major media organizations and we never knew ahead of time when camera teams or newspaper reporters would be in the room.

I was standing on the platform with Pastor John waiting to give some announcements when the crowing began. We both looked at each other, astounded and shocked. John whispered to me,

"Mary Audrey, what is she doing? Oh God, oh God, thank heaven "they" aren't here tonight!" By "they" he meant the crews from such as CBC, NBC, CNN and the BBC. He walked over to the edge of the stage, looked down at the lady and calling her by name said, "What's happening? Do you know what you're doing?" "Of course," she replied. "It's the Lord saying 'Wake up, wake up! It's a new day."

Now, some probably thought that was a pretty ridiculous way to bring a prophetic encouragement from the Lord but I guarantee it had much more impact and would be remembered much longer than some prophetic person speaking into a microphone and saying," The Lord says, be aware my people, a new day is at hand." Like it or it, the Spirit of God was certainly bringing the church into a "new day" and He wanted us to recognize it. We also knew the validity of the word because we knew the spiritual integrity of the woman who delivered it.

We began to ask people what was happening with them – what were they thinking or feeling when it appeared that the Holy Spirit was moving upon them. Usually we would wait until the encounter with the Lord seemed to be finished and then ask for an explanation so we could understand.

One evening we observed an older, sedate, British, Church of England bishop rolling around and around on the floor holding his ribs and howling with laughter. It seemed so out of character for him to be this demonstrative. When he could finally sit up we asked, "What on earth was happening with you?" With tears in his eyes, he shared that as a young child he had been sent away from home to a very exclusive boys' school in England. He was seldom with his parents and he had practically a non-existent relationship with his father who was very rigid, preoccupied and distant. With no concept of a father's love, the lonely boy grew up to be a very private, unemotional, shy and distant man, even though he excelled academically, entered the ministry and eventually became a man of authority in his denomination.

That evening, at the revival meeting, the Holy Spirit fell upon him during prayer time and as he rested upon the floor, he found himself having the most marvellous experience. He saw himself as a little boy in the presence of his Heavenly Father who, holding him in His arms, wrestled him to the floor while relentlessly tickling his ribs, kissing him on his neck and hugging him ferociously. The little boy wiggled and jiggled and howled with laughter just as children do today when their parents engage in joyful play and interaction with them. He encountered a real father's love. I am persuaded that more healing happened in that bishop's soul in the half-hour on the floor with the Lord than could be achieved through numerous counselling sessions. Needless to say, when that man returned home to his church family, the people found they had a transformed leader.

THE WEIGHTY PRESENCE OF GOD

Along with laughter being part of this move of God, another phenomena was that people were "slain in the Spirit" as a regular happening.

For those readers who are not familiar with this term it refers to the fact that many times when in the Lord's presence, often while being prayed for, a person will fall to the floor or slump over in their chair. Another term for this could be "resting in the Spirit". It may appear that one has fainted but that is not so. The majority of the time you are very aware of what's going on around you. Instead of becoming all analytical, I have encouraged people to say, "Lord, what have you got me in this position for that you couldn't do when I was upright?"

During this time people often experience a deep peace; healing in their bodies; have revelatory visions; and find in hindsight that it was a preparation for a future ministry to which they were being called.

It's as if He has you pinned there for moments of time, with Him in control of your faculties. Many times, for me, it feels like a big soft elephant is sitting on my chest and while I think I can get up whenever I want to, most of the time I choose to cooperate and stay there until His presence lifts. I believe that when people sense that weightiness upon them, it is actually the Kabod which is the Glory of God resting upon them. One of the meanings of Kabod is the weighty presence of God.

While in the majority of instances people stay in this position from a few minutes to half an hour or more, some remain being deeply impacted by the Lord for several hours. We hesitate to force someone to get up too soon, and often have a ministry team person sit with them, quietly blessing them until their session with the Lord is finished.

A testimony came from one husband who reported that his wife was in that place for two days, unable to leave their hotel room. Another pastor and I had to take one lady back to her hotel in a wheel chair. She had been resting in the Spirit for several hours during the evening meeting and when it was time for everyone to go home we couldn't rouse her so we lifted her into the wheelchair, then into the car, then into the chair again at the hotel. The staff at reception thought she was just drunk so they let us wheel her to her room where we plopped her on to her bed, covered her up, blessed her and departed. Next morning, bright and early, she arrived for the morning meeting feeling as though she had been away for an invigorating spa treatment.

For newcomers, this manifestation can be quite foreign especially if it does not happen in their particular church setting. "Why are they falling over?" they would ask. I used to try and give succinct answers and explain everything but finally got comfortable enough to just reply, "Because they can't stand up". I couldn't presume to know what the Lord wanted to do in a person's life. One evening a family of five from another nation stood before me on the prayer line and the father said to me very firmly, "We don't fall over!" and I replied, "That's OK, I don't do windows". At that, as I lifted my hand to bless them, all five collapsed to the floor and remained here for some time. I was as surprised as they were!

COMPARING EXPERIENCES

One of our challenges is that we tend to compare ourselves to others and their experiences. With this issue of being slain in the Spirit, some fall to the floor, some do not. I have seen people touched deeply by the power of God and remain standing, lost in Him, for long periods of time. I like to call it "being slain standing up". We should not judge the validity of what is happening within a person based on whether they fall over or not. There can be a tendency to assume that if a person does not fall down, they are somehow less spiritual than others or they are quenching or resisting the Holy Spirit. Believing this, people feel very self-conscious and somehow less acceptable to God. They think, "What's the matter with me?"

59

I remember, during that first week of revival in 1994, being in a prayer line with about fifty other pastors. We were called forward to receive an impartation from Randy Clark. Standing with my hands outstretched and my eyes closed I was aware when he came by and touched my forehead for a moment before moving along to the next person. After a few minutes I opened my eyes, looked around and was embarrassed to see that I was the only one of the whole group still standing. I felt like a giant wart! The "what's the matter with me" syndrome hit like a ton of bricks and I had some long conversations with God about it. After all, wasn't I one of the leaders in the house? Shouldn't I at least "look" spiritual in front of others? In the beginning, many thought that this manifestation carried great significance and validation. In time I realized that this was a pretty bad attitude as the Lord assured me repeatedly that I was not resisting Him one bit, but that we all respond to Him differently.

The experience helped me bring assurance to many others who remain standing alone in a crowd. Simply put, "some do and some don't". Our senior pastor, John Arnott, stood like a giant oak tree all through the exuberant early years of the revival. He still does. His wife, Carol, was like a limp noodle who had to learn to stand in the anointing in order to minister to others. She still, to this day, is extremely sensitive to the Holy Spirit and responsive physically to the Lord's presence.

IT'S NOT ALWAYS WHAT THE EYE CAN SEE

We can never second-guess what is happening with someone from outward appearances. A church in Florida had heard about the happenings in Toronto and decided to bless their pastor by sending him north for a week with the admonition to bring "everything" back home to them. Pastor M did so and faithfully attended all the day sessions and the evening meetings but experienced nothing, personally, all week long. He had no sensing of God's presence, no reactions, no resting in the Spirit, no unusual joy – nothing. He was extremely disappointed and concerned about going home feeling as "blah" as when he had left and with nothing to give his congregation.

Arriving home late Saturday evening, he was concerned about facing his people on the Sunday morning with no great testimony. However, one thing he had observed while in Toronto was the habit of welcoming the Lord with the words, "Come, Holy Spirit" and so he decided that was all he could say and when he did so, "bang" - all heaven broke loose in that church. Unknowingly, he had received an impartation to carry a revival anointing and it was released to his congregation as soon as he returned home.

I understand that joy and laughter burst forth, people were spontaneously slain in the Spirit, physical healings occurred, and the altar area was full as people seriously rededicated themselves to Christ. It was not the usual one hour church service! He too realized a drastic change in his own heart and with an accelerated hunger for God he led his people into being a vital influence in the community.

A NOISY PEOPLE AND NEW SOUNDS

Another feature of the revival which generated considerable controversy was the explosion of new sounds. While many full gospel and Pentecostal type churches are accustomed to the occasional "Amen" or "Praise the Lord" during their services what began to be heard at our church was different, to say the least. Most churches are not likely to appreciate people in the congregation bursting out with loud joy in the middle of the meeting. We were getting used to handling the spontaneous laughter and could even preach over the noise. When it was of the Spirit it didn't annoy, irritate or distract us. It would be highly contagious and at times I wondered if people were just enjoying themselves. We began to be able to discern the difference between what the Lord was generating and people being silly or attention seeking. Sometimes it would be a single person disturbing the meeting and we would send someone from the ministry team to quieten them down.

However, one evening the Lord had a laugh on us. We had as our guest speaker a famous, denominational leader from England who was known for his amazing teaching on the Grace of God.

He was a very proper gentleman who oversaw a number of evangelical churches and we wondered if he would appreciate the revival atmosphere that permeated the Toronto meetings. He had never been to Toronto before. I was hosting the meeting that night and my "controller anointing" was in full swing. After all, we wanted this prestigious man to like and approve of us so he would take a good report back home with him.

After about ten minutes into his sermon, a section of about thirty people at the far right side of the room spontaneously began to laugh loudly in unison. This caught the speaker totally by surprise; you could tell by the look on his face. I gave a "raised eyebrow and nod of the head" signal to one of our security staff indicating that he was to get over there as fast as possible and settle those people down – now! Decorum reigned again and the speaker carried on with his message for about another ten minutes.

Then, horrors, from the far left side of the room came the sound of laughter from another large group. The "raised eyebrow and nod of the head" signal sent the security person over to that section to bring things into order. All was well again for the next ten or fifteen minutes until, as if led by an invisible orchestra conductor, a whole center section of several hundred people seated behind me burst out in hilarious laughter and I got the hint.

The Lord was up to something so why not just leave it alone. Our speaker was finally able to finish his message, with big smiles on his face too, and thoroughly enjoyed the next few days of his visit encountering the Spirit's presence in a refreshing way for him.

Other sounds would burst forth from people. Sounds like "HO", "WOAH-O-O-O-O", and "WOW" were heard frequently and even sounds like roaring lions and others that resembled dogs barking. The temptation at times was to try and validate the manifestations scripturally – to make them more acceptable to our religious mindsets, I guess. Not really a good idea; one can mistakenly try to make anything fit with the Bible but it could be totally out of context.

Having said that, however, it is interesting to note that there is a reference to barking dogs in Isaiah 56:10 which states, *"For Israel's watchmen are blind, the whole lot of them. They have no idea what's going on. They're dogs without sense enough to bark, lazy dogs, dreaming in the sun."* (MSG). Considering that watchmen are those who need to be alert, warning when danger is coming, could it be that intercessors in the church today are to be as watchmen, seeing what is going on and standing on guard, as it were, and barking – giving warning when necessary? Would it be stretching things too much to consider that the revival barking signified a call to intercession?

One of the most common sounds over the years has been "HO". Various dictionaries define the word as: calling attention to; urging onward; expressing surprise or joy. It also means to "hold on".

In Isaiah 55:1, it is at the beginning of a call, an invitation, for spiritually thirsty and hungry people to come and partake freely of the Lord's provisions. It is an invitation to Abundant Life!

Two different versions express it this way:

HO, everyone that thirsteth, come to the waters, and he that hath no money; come ye, buy and eat; yea, come, buy wine and milk without money and without price. KJV

WAIT and listen, everyone who is thirsty! Come to the waters; and he who has no money, come, buy and eat! Yes, come and buy {priceless, spiritual} wine and milk without money and without price {simply for the self-surrender that accepts the blessing}. AMP

Without a doubt, many thousands of spiritually thirsty people have responded to the "HO" over the years at the watering hole now known as Catch The Fire. The sound still goes forth.

INEXPLICABLE OCCURENCES

Many times there was simply the sovereign, outward, manifest presence of the Holy Spirit. Sounds, like that of an angelic choir, would be heard accompanying the worship team. A heavy dew or mist, like a cloud, would rest over sections of the sanctuary. You could feel the moisture on your hands and face and you knew it wasn't produced by the air conditioners or a leaky roof on a rainy day. There were times you could literally see, from the platform, a cloud-like form resting over the heads of people and moving from one section of the room to another. Sometimes there was such a "thickness" in the air that you could almost hold the weight of His presence in your hands.

During one season, the Lord chose to do miracles in people's mouths by changing their amalgam tooth fillings to gold. That really created critical controversy! The big question was, "Why would God waste His energy on something as trivial as that when there are so many other needs in the world!" I have no idea, except to say that it was surely a sign that made people wonder! The ones who were really thrilled were those who got the gold fillings. One woman's dentist was upset with her, believing that she had gone elsewhere for treatment.

My scepticism disappeared while checking a lady's testimony that she had received a gold tooth. I was standing with her on the platform, a camera filming over my shoulder while I shone a flashlight into her open mouth. Yes, there was gold molar but the amazement came when I watched another molar, with an old-looking filling, transform to bright gold before my eyes and before the camera, too.

There is no ending to the stories, the testimonies that are pouring out from the revival. In the next chapter I will share a few of them as well as look at some of the "interesting" people that were attracted to the meetings.

Chapter Six

OIL, OVARIES & ODDITIES

There are simply not enough pages here to report on all of the stories of physical and emotional healing, restorations of relationships, freshened vision for Kingdom living and the startling, humbling revelation that God is God - we're not!

TIMES OF WONDER

During one of our women's conferences, a young wife and mother, who I will name Terry, came from England. One of the first things to happen was that, during worship one evening, oil began to form and cover her hands and the tops of her feet. It was not self-produced, spread on, or simply a flow of copious perspiration. I felt that it was an indication of a healing anointing and so had a ministry team member accompany her as she prayed for the sick.

In the meeting was an American woman brought by her father from a hospital in Chicago.

She had just undergone emergency, extensive cardiac surgery with a resulting poor prognosis for her future. Desperately wanting to come to the conference, she checked herself out of the hospital and convinced her Dad to bring her to Toronto where she believed she would have an encounter with her Healer, Jesus. Her father made a bed for her in the back of his station wagon so she could travel the distance. Hardly able to walk, let alone hold herself upright, she sat slumped in a wheelchair looking grey, tiny and weak. I took Terry over to her. When those drippy, oily hands were laid on her chest, suddenly healthy colour returned to her cheeks, her eyes brightened, she felt a release of life and energy within her. Getting out of the wheelchair, she never sat in it again and when it was time to return home, she rode in the front seat with her Dad. I understand that she returned to her very active job in a veterinarian's clinic shortly later, healed and restored to life.

There's more to the story about Terry, however. One evening, for an hour or more, she lay quietly on the floor at the side of the platform away from the crowd. It appeared as though she was sleeping, she was so quiet. She was lost in personal worship and aware of God's loving presence. Finally, sitting up and preparing to return to her seat, she felt something in her hand. Opening it, she was flabbergasted to see a gold ring set with a large, brilliant, solitaire diamond. The ring fit her perfectly. How it got there no one can explain because no person had come near to her while she was on the floor nor had anyone put anything into her hand. It was definitely a supernatural manifestation from the Holy Spirit.

This amazing gift was especially wonderful and meaningful for her because, earlier in the year she had lost the stone out of her engagement ring which saddened her greatly.

I lost track of Terry until recently, a number of years later, her husband introduced himself to me while I was speaking at a conference in another city. He told me that Terry still had her beautiful ring and that she was still ministering healing, the oil still flowing, on a regular basis.

MISTAKEN IDENTITY

Sometimes, I think the Lord chuckles at the way we handle things. One evening, when it was my turn to speak at one of the revival meetings, I received a word of knowledge that there were those in the meeting who needed to be healed from ovarian cysts. Calling those who knew they had such conditions forward for ministry, I moved off of the platform to lay hands on those who responded to the call. There seemed to be around thirty individuals come to the prayer line. I carried the microphone with me. This night rather than specifically praying for each one, I moved quickly from one person to the next, not looking at their faces but focussing on their abdominal area. Laying one hand on their mid-sections I directly spoke to the cysts commanding them to be removed in the name of Jesus of Nazareth. People in the congregation could hear what I was saying because of the mike. Well, as I neared the end of the line, all of a sudden I burst out with, "You don't have ovaries! You don't belong here!" and looking up saw that I had my hands on an Asian man's stomach area. What a moment of embarrassment, as ushers escorted the man away. We came to realize that some ethnic groups would respond to every type of altar call offered, no matter what it was, just in case something good would be imparted.

LONGING LEADERS

During the early years of the revival many well-known personalities from around the world would quietly arrive. They represented many ministries and denominations, including television. Some came, just out of curiosity to check things out, others to personally receive a refreshing touch from the Holy Spirit. We would recognize them at times, sitting toward the back of the room. Trying to be incognito and casual, they were not dressed in their usual 3-piece suits, nice shirts and ties, but in jeans, t-shirts or track pants, frequently wearing sun-glasses. Often we would recognize them in a different position, out of their chairs doing "carpet time", a term we would smilingly use when people would rest on the floor after being slain in the Spirit. Wanting to honour their privacy, we seldom made reference to the fact they were there.

I was present when one prominent apostolic leader from the States, while speaking at a large Washington conference, gave testimony about his experience in Toronto. He drove there himself, alone, just to check out what he had heard about us. Was the Holy Spirit really moving there or was the whole thing just being generated by a bunch of over-zealous people? He related that after finding a place in the parking lot, he got out of the car and promptly fell to the ground immediately encountering the presence and power of God. No one was around to help him – he was late and everyone was already in the meeting. He literally crawled to the automatic doors, through them into the church, and manoeuvred himself to a seat in the last row of chairs. He needed no other proof that, indeed, the sovereign Lord was present and had a life-changing few days.

REVIVAL ATTRACTS "INTERESTING PEOPLE"

Right from the beginning we were dubiously blessed with the arrival of a number of self-appointed "apostles" and "prophets". Most of them were what we call "lone rangers", accountable to no one but themselves. They all felt they should have the platform to direct us or bring a "word from God". My first experience with such a person happened during the third week of the renewal, in 1994. I was having lunch in the little hotdog café at the church when a very authoritarian stranger, a woman, came up to me and giving me the once-over, declared, "I am an apostle, you know! Where do you want me to sit in there?" I thought to myself, "What's the big deal?" Being somewhat ignorant about ministry protocol in those days, I gave her a blank look, sort of shrugged my shoulders and said, "I don't know. It doesn't really matter. There are plenty of seats to choose from as you're here early." She huffed off, seemingly quite disgusted with my lack of recognition of her office. I never saw her again.

A nerve-wracking situation occurred one evening in our big new sanctuary when I was hosting an evening meeting. While I was facing one side of the room, this huge, hairy guy walked up behind me onto the stage and grabbing the extra microphone, he began to release words over the congregation. I like to describe him as combination of "one from the back side of the mountain", Hoss from the TV program "Ponderosa" and one of the stars from the current "Duck Dynasty" series. It took a minute for the security team to realize what was happening, get up to the platform and firmly remove him.

You may be shocked that a church would have to resort to such tactics as having a security team. This became necessary because we had so many challenging people come with their own agendas, refusing night after night to comply with requests and house rules - i.e. please sit down when you're asked to; please leave the platform; please don't interrupt the speaker; please go to the back of the room as you're causing a distraction; please don't harass the ladies; or please don't look for handouts, etc. Some were seriously mentally disturbed, one even punching a ministry worker in the face, knocking her off of her feet, and causing painful bruising. Needless to say, the police were called in on this one. Some had to be given formal letters stating that they weren't welcome in the building and if they still chose to be there, the police would be called.

PERSISTENCE PAYS OFF

Groups of extremely hungry, enthusiastic believers from a particular Asian nation would come fairly regularly, usually around 125 at a time. They would arrive very early for all of the meetings heading straight for the front sections so they could be "close to the anointing" where they assumed it would be. They held the particular belief that if they got very close to, or could touch, the pastoral leaders or guest speakers there would be an increase in the blessings they would receive. One evening as I was sitting in that "row of anointing" awaiting my turn to go to the platform, I suddenly felt a tight grip like a rope around my left ankle. I couldn't shake it off no matter how hard I tried so, looking to discover what it was, I was stunned to see a hand wrapped around my ankle. It was attached to a little body which was attached to another little body, which was attached to another little body and so on. I realized that about a dozen little bodies were holding on to one another in a daisy-chain formation stretching across the aisle and under the seats until some "anointed" person's appendage could be touched and an impartation released.

For too long I was extremely annoyed and critical of these darling people who just wanted God so much that they thought nothing of pushing in and interrupting team workers as they prayed for someone else and would personally return over and over for more laying on of hands and ministry.

When receiving ministry, they were like bouncing balls falling to the floor and popping up again for "more", over and over again. We finally decided to hold information sessions for these particular groups to explain our Toronto church protocol and our version of good manners. Among other things, I would tell them that the Holy Spirit wanted to bless them deeply and that it would be beneficial if they remained resting in His Presence for awhile when lying on the floor. "What a novel idea," they said, and so, thereafter, complied.

One particular session remains indelibly imprinted in my memory. I became aware of another cultural difference. Over one hundred smiling men politely fell to the floor in orderly fashion, one after the other, like dominoes. As they rested in the Spirit, their bodies began, almost simultaneously, to manifest exuberant toots of joy and release. I was probably the only embarrassed one there..

Eventually, I became convicted over my crummy attitude and with repentance came a love and acceptance which brought great enjoyment over the years as I was privileged to get to know them and welcome them to the church. We North Americans could stand to be so spiritually aggressive and openly hungry!

OTHER AGENDAS

As well as spiritual hungry believers, people from the "dark side" arrived. Some would slip in to the building when no meeting was happening and hide artifacts around the place, such as strips of cassette tape loaded with curses. We would find weird objects like little dolls and strange jewellery stuck in the baskets of greenery which hung from the balcony at the back of the sanctuary. We actually discovered ribbons of cassette tape placed all around the outside perimeter of the building hidden in the grass, flower beds and bushes.

Some of these people would position themselves around the room or as close to the stage as possible, exhibiting strange hand language. We would find individuals who were not approved members of the ministry team praying with vulnerable people using the new age technique of "massaging their auras". Needless to say, our intercessors were kept very busy.

Vagrants would arrive needing a bed. They usually began their stories with, "God sent me". Some actually hid in the bathrooms, standing on the toilet seats so their feet couldn't be seen under the doors by the ushers when they were checking the building at closing time. They also found great places to hide in back hallways, stairwells and storage closets. They wanted a place to sleep. You may think we were totally inhospitable but our insurance plan simply did not cover us for over-night guests. One nightshift security guard, upon finding such people hiding in the church, would drive them to a nearby hotel and deposit them in the lobby.

ALL DID NOT SPEAK WELL OF US

Another thing we had to live with were the false accusations. Cruel critics mocked and labelled us as a weird cult, as deceivers, as damaging to the body of Christ. They warned people to stay away from our church and their influence created considerable fear. For the most part, they accused us from a distance, never actually attending one of the meetings.

One local pastor was devastated while listening to the radio as he drove back to Canada late at night after a meeting in Buffalo, NY. He had the dial turned to a Christian station and was shocked to hear what was being played. Someone had somehow altered (doctored) the words of a sermon spoken by Carol Arnott and had produced an ugly, heretical version of her message. This was being broadcast internationally. Knowing Carol well, her love of the Word, her quiet gentleness, her integrity, and her passion for Jesus, he began to weep. Knowing she would never say such things, he had to stop the car on the side of the road until he recovered from the shock.

The articles and books written, the broadcasts and sermons preached against us, were painful. However, instead of reacting with the need to defend and retaliate, the leaders continually chose to forgive and bless the critics. We have seen some turn around, repent for their slander of the revival, ask our forgiveness and be so personally touched by God that they are now leading revival churches themselves.

Sometimes we mistakenly think we have to defend the Lord, but it's not necessary. He can look after Himself quite well. I recall an event that occurred during an early revival conference in England. A denominational leader, who was also an author and broadcaster, had written numerous articles for a large Christian publication denouncing the Toronto Blessing. Knowing he would be welcomed to the platform, he came to the meeting with the firm intent to castigate and rebuke us publically. While sitting in his seat during worship, the power of God fell upon him, not only drastically shaking him from head to toe, but also speaking strong words of correction to his heart. He went to the platform crying like a baby and blubbering into the microphone he asked for our forgiveness and spoke blessings to us all. Needless to say, his next magazine article was quite different and very favourable toward the revival.

What is making me extremely thankful these days is having opportunities to speak with an increasing number of people about some of the things which really happened in Toronto. They are ones who were doubtful, concerned and somewhat fearful as a result of listening to the "nay-sayers." Now, they want to know for themselves, not through second or third-hand reports.

From the very beginning, in 1994, we were aware of the need to provide a vehicle for safe ministry to the thousands who arrived on our doorstep. Read on to see some of the ways we attempted to do this.

Chapter Seven

TRAINING THE TROOPS

We knew it was necessary from the very beginning of revival to develop a good ministry team. We have always strongly believed in the body ministering to the body, not just leaving prayer up to the "the man of power for the hour."

The role of our prayer/ministry team is to point people to Jesus. We want to help others have a supernatural encounter with God and His love in such a way they are changed forever. The team helps create a healing environment where the Holy Spirit is welcome and where those who come can feel safe enough to open up their hearts to God.

Before the revival began we had about thirty, who trained in healing prayer, were able to do altar ministry usually after the Sunday services and during the occasional, larger, yearly events. This group grew to 300 when we began to have large conferences with thousands attending. We averaged out to seventy-five or so for the evening meetings in the first number of years. Nowadays, there are Catch the Fire and "river type" churches around the world. People don't have to travel as much to the Toronto location but can be a part of revival reality closer to home. Our ministry team has reduced in size but a large number are still on hand for the bigger events, many having faithfully served for the past twenty years.

THE NEED FOR RESPONSIBLE OVERSIGHT

In the early years, Christians from many denominations and countries wanted to pray with others as part of the ministry team. They said they were accustomed to ministering to people at home and, offering their services, thought they would just be able to do the same with us. Some were rather upset with us when we said, "No thank you. Why don't you just receive for yourself."

Wanting to protect the people who came to be blessed, we needed to know who was serving amongst us and so we became, not exclusive, but definitely choosey. How were we to know the true track-record of the "eager beavers", some of whom had their own agendas, just itching to lay hands on a warm body? We tried our best to eliminate the chance of random, out-of-sight, back hall pray-ers as well as parking lot and hotel room ministers. Night after night we implored people to refuse ministry from anyone not wearing a designated team badge.

We wanted to train people with the same vision and goals – not clones, but those with hearts in unity. 2 Tim 2:2 exhorts us to, *"pass on the truths to trustworthy men and women."* Most importantly, we looked for those with the heart of a servant, their significance coming from God not from being on the team.

Consequently, we developed an in-depth personal application form and questionnaire for anyone desiring to be on the team. We also required that a pastor's reference and approval letter be attached. This was mandatory for anyone, from our own church family as well as elsewhere. The application was carefully and prayerfully considered before we accepted anyone. Sometimes it was a challenge for people to obtain approval from their pastors if they didn't like what was happening in the meetings. These ones usually didn't join the team as we did not want to create division or encourage others to be rebellious toward their leaders. Many surrendered to this refusal and prayerfully waited, interceding until their leader had a change of heart and released them to join us.

As well, we chose to receive those who were more mature believers, rather than novices and logically, they had to understand and speak English.

CLEAN HANDS AND A PURE HEART

We also needed to assess if there were "un-dealt-with" sin issues in one's life. This was usually accomplished through "reading between the lines" on the application form, noting attitudes and discernment. Did the person still have major unhealed areas of rejection, control, unforgiveness, and especially sexual sin? We knew that such stuff could spill over onto people when hands were laid on them during ministry time.

The error of not being diligent in this preliminary task in one case caused an unfortunate situation to occur. We began getting negative reports from a number of women who were prayed for by a visiting pastor on the team. He was just a great guy, very likeable, and compassionate and because he was known by other leaders, we made an exception and bypassed the application form for him. The reports came in over several days. The women were unknown to each other and so we knew the complaints were not a setup to discredit the guy. All had the same reaction - that of feeling "slimed" i.e., sexually unclean, after being prayed for by this man.

Two of our male pastors took the fellow aside privately, explained the problem, and he was devastated. He confessed sexual impropriety that had occurred years before which had never been dealt with, just hidden away. Now at the enemy's choice of time, the fruit of that sin, manifesting as uncleanness, flowed out of him. The man was broken-hearted. He truly repented, received forgiveness and cleansing and immediately returned home to share with his wife and take an extended time away from the ministry until restored again by the Lord.

MINISTERING WITH THE HELP OF THE SPIRIT

Even for the visiting teams, we conducted training on hearing God's voice for guidance in ministering to others. Needing to be sensitive and obedient to the promptings of the Holy Spirit, they found more fruit in their ministry when they prayed according to what He was showing them rather than according to their own agendas.

They also learned how to pray for healing; how to recognize and use the gifts of the Spirit listed by Paul in 1 Cor.12:7-10, especially prophecy and the revelatory abilities of word of knowledge, word of wisdom and discerning of spirits; and how to pray the Word, i.e. biblical truths drawn from the storehouse within them. They had to learn to minister quickly but compassionately in a renewal setting which was not conducive to in-depth counselling or deliverance. They learned how to quietly sit with ones who were resting in the Spirit and simply bless what the Lord was accomplishing within them.

Because praying for the opposite gender can be a sensitive issue, we preferred that the ministry be done in pairs if possible and, for the most part, men would pray with men and women with women.

As many people who received prayer were overcome by the Holy Spirit, to avoid injury, a catcher would stand behind them unless they were already seated, kneeling or lying on the floor.

Our ideal was to pray for each person who stood on the prayer lines. Consequently, with many hundreds waiting, we ministered many evenings until well after midnight.

The enthusiasm, faithfulness and long-term commitment of the team was outstanding and I believe this prayer team was a major factor in many people having a meaningful and lasting encounter with God.

To best describe the heart of our church toward those who came to be blessed, and who still do come after all these years, I leave with you Pastor John Arnott's introduction to our Prayer Ministry Team Training Manual.

"These are privileged days we are living in, where the Lord is pouring out His Holy Spirit across the world – to every nation and people group. We, at the Toronto Airport Christian Fellowship, have been blessed beyond measure to be a "well" of Living Water for people all over the world to come and drink here.

The mission statement of this church, before the outbreak of this move of the Spirit on January 20th, 1994 was, "that we may walk in God's love and then give it away." We have now changed our mission statement to include "to Toronto and the world." This, more than ever, expresses our heart to continue to minister out of God's love.

We desire to be good stewards of what has been entrusted to us and to minister in and from God's love with excellence. Hence, we have taken considerable care in how we train our Prayer Ministry Team.

We wish to emphasize that we do not consider ourselves to be either experts or that the principles in this manual to be the only way. We are still learning as we go along. As we have had well over 3 million people that have stood on the lines to receive prayer we have learned the importance of some safeguards and boundaries mentioned in this manual.

We trust that you will find many principles in our training that will hold true in any setting. Most importantly that we are to minister in the power of His love. We hold the message of God's love, mercy, grace, the cross, repentance and forgiveness of sins in high value and are truths that we live by. However, there are many guidelines that are necessary for this setting that may not be necessary or appropriate in other settings.

We trust that you will find our Prayer Ministry Training of help to you as you continue learning and growing in the love of God and giving it away to others."[2]

I trust that this gives you a wider perspective of some of the ingredients of the Toronto Blessing as the revival was called. We would have preferred it if people had called it the Father's Blessing.

[2] Prayer Ministry Team Training Manual,
(Toronto: Toronto Airport Christian Fellowship, 2004) Introduction.

Chapter Eight

THE CHALLENGE–
WHO'S IN CHARGE?

This book on the Toronto Blessing has been written from one participant's point of view and is not based on a set of rules or regulations or an established revival culture. We had to learn one step at time and obey the Lord, one step at a time. We did realize that what was happening in Toronto could not be packaged or copied. Unconfirmed, but I have heard that in the 1990s about 7,000 churches in the UK tried to reproduce the revival that was happening in Canada. Many "petered out" because they wanted another Toronto and tried to imitate what was happening there. Now, a number of years later many of these fellowships are rising again with their own unique flavours as their leaders listen to the Holy Spirit's directions.

We at the Toronto church should never be considered an authority on any of this. It would be too easy to formulate a Doctrine of Revival and put barriers around it according to our own particular brand and experience. The biggest challenge for us was to trust God, take our hands off, trust Him for His wisdom, and learn to obey His voice. Obviously that meant we needed to learn how to hear and recognize it.

WHOSE CHURCH IS IT?

A comment was once made that we believers need to give the church back to God, but what does that look like? We are so used to our own denominational paradigms that we think we're totally pleasing Him; so comfortable in our own parameters and institutional boxes. Man-made traditions and programs may seem safe, people-pleasing, undisturbing and sensitive to those who we hope are seeking God, but may not be anointed. As the Spirit fell upon us, we were challenged in these areas.

I remember a Sunday morning in the early years of the revival when a prophet by the name of Graham Cooke spoke an encouraging but strong word to the church family. Remembering the biblical account of Moses leading the children of Israel to the Promised Land, he reminded us that whenever the leaders saw the pillar of cloud, which signified the Lord's presence, move on, then the people were to set out again on their trek following Him (Exodus 40:36).

Graham exhorted us to "keep very loose structures" and to be prepared to "move with the cloud". We know he didn't mean that we shouldn't have a building and so forth but that we needed to be very flexible and willing to follow the Lord's agenda.

GIVING UP CONTROL

Many who are "gate keepers" i.e., pastors, ministers and church leaders, can tend to be very nervous about letting the Holy Spirit run with His agenda, especially in regular Sunday services. I know, personally, what security it gave me to have the program all planned in advance with no surprises. That is finally getting weaned out of me.

Losing control is the big issue.

One Sunday morning we simply could not get out of worship. It was a glorious time of pouring our hearts out in songs of intimate adoration and praise. I think it would have been almost a sin to shut the worship down in order to get on with the rest of the program, i.e. announcements, offering, and the sermon. The Spirit was deeply touching people's hearts. The service began at 10:30 a.m. as usual and we were still worshipping by noon. One disgruntled man was heard remarking as he left shortly after 12:00 p.m., "Hmmph - I sure didn't come here to sing songs for two hours!" Obviously, we were not "on the same page" as we were doing much more than simply singing songs!

On another occasion, the Lord led us to enter into a time of healing ministry early in the worship and again, we never did get to the "important" matters that day.

Again, giving up control is a huge issue.

I think a big question is "how much do we really want revival?" As a leader, I would really be afraid to say, "No", even if I didn't understand it or it didn't fit into my particular religious structure. I remember the indignant attitudes expressed by a number of ministers as the River began to flow, too close for their comfort. Their people were confused and saddened as many of them had tasted the revival goodness of God and longed for their own pastors to welcome the Spirit into their churches. "We don't want any of that Holy Spirit stuff in here!" their leaders declared. Two fears can often dictate a leader's decision: fear of losing control and fear of losing finances if people leave.

CHOOSING TO WALK AN UNFAMILIAR ROAD

No doubt there are pastors reading this book who are really wanting to take their people to a deeper place in the Lord. Seriously welcoming the Holy Spirit into your church will have to be a choice, made without apologies and with a firm resolve to carry on, especially when you discover that everyone won't want to walk with you in this. Fortunately, only a small number from our congregation departed after the revival began in Toronto; however, one California based church dropped from a thousand members to three hundred, almost overnight. Another smaller fellowship lost all but the eight who were some of the pastor's family members.

With their hunger for God unabated, these pastors stayed 100% committed even though having to walk in uncharted ways. Praise God, both of these fellowships have since grown phenomenally, overflowing with enthusiastic, Kingdom-minded believers. I heard John Arnott declare many times, when asked for explanations, "We have no 'grid' for this." Abraham had no "grid", no road map as he obeyed God, chose to make a drastic life change and set out for a new, unknown land.

> *"The Lord had said to Abram, "Leave your country, your people and your father's household and go to the land I will show you." So Abram left, as the Lord had told him...he was seventy-five years old when he set out from Haran...they set out for the land of Canaan and they arrived there."*
>
> —Genesis 12:1,4a,5b NIV

> *By faith Abraham, when called to go to a place he would later receive as his inheritance, obeyed and*

went, even though he did not know where he was going.

—Hebrews 11:8 NIV

You may remember that Joshua and Caleb stood firmly against the tide of public opinion, almost losing their lives. Read about this adventure in Numbers 13:1-14:24.

The faith of these forerunners, Abraham, Joshua and Caleb, held them steady. The same kind of faith will hold you steady as you go on to new territory with the Spirit of God as your guide.

Undoubtedly, stepping into the river of revival will bring challenging choices and bold decisions. The one who is an apostolic pioneer of a church may have an easier time. You are the leader; the people joined you, something drawing them to your leadership; they can either stay or leave; you don't require their permission to flow as God leads you (and yes, you still need to have healthy relationships and be accountable to others in the body, not walking as an independent "lone-ranger").

On the other hand, if you are one who has been hired by a church, a denominational board or institutional committee, the challenge can be quite different. You joined them and are under their authority and receive direction and approval for most church activities. Therefore much wisdom and sensitivity is needed as you guide your flock into new spiritual territory.

The serious question to be asked is, "who is leading who?" Is it the Holy Spirit or the dictates of men?

GIVE TO THE HUNGRY

In 2 Timothy 2:6 Paul tells his young protégé Timothy, *"the hard-working farmer is the first partaker of the fruit."* As you choose to move into renewal in your own life and ministry first, there'll be an impartation to those who are hungry. In other words, you receive first and then you can pass it on.

I remember when I began to teach about the Gifts of the Spirit at a time, some years ago, when such topics were controversial in mainline denominational churches. I was so enthusiastic and wanted everyone I met to get a hold of these truths. I couldn't understand why some were just simply not interested, frequently moaning and groaning to the woman who was my mentor. She gave me some excellent advice which stands true especially in these days of revival, "Quit trying to prove things to those who really aren't interested... just feed the hungry!"

Just feed the hungry! I recall the comments I made to a Spirit-filled Anglican pastor as we met for lunch one day several years before the Toronto revival began. He seemed depressed and after he had shared his concern, I was shocked as I heard the words that came from my mouth. He was an extremely long-suffering, mercy-motivated man who cared for a small congregation. Many of the parishioners sat stiffly with arms folded and sober, non-smiling set faces as Sunday after Sunday they came for their one-hour weekly ritual. Their joy seemed to be non-existent. My friend, the parish priest, was becoming drained and discouraged as he wore himself out trying to please them all.

At the same time, there were about twenty others who had received the baptism in the Holy Spirit. They were so alive, hungry and keen, wanting "more" in worship, teaching and mentoring in the life of the Spirit. They needed feeding and encouragement to move on with God and were beginning to go elsewhere to receive it.

They definitely were not getting it at home base as their pastor was blinded and hobbled by the control of the long-established ones. He was afraid that he was losing the "alive" ones.

Unaccustomed to speaking so directly and boldly to a church leader, I surprised myself when I said, "How long are you going to pour out your life to the lowest common denominator. They've made it clear that they have no intention of changing. There are ones in your midst who are starving!" That surprised him, too. It sounded harsh, but he heard it as a wake-up-call. Immediately, he began to "father" the hungry ones and interact with like-minded pastors and believers in other communities. Entering into a personal revival, it was not long after that he left the "frozen" place and ventured out into prison ministry, into work with minority groups, and into vibrant ministry outside the old four walls, feeding the spiritually hungry.

WALK IN GOD'S LOVE AND GIVE IT AWAY

This has been the heart of Catch the Fire since the church began. In closing this chapter, one thing I should mention is that there was never any sense of ownership with what was happening at Toronto. As said earlier in the book, we never ever wanted the revival to be called the "Toronto Blessing". That title originated in England and stuck. We would have much preferred it to be known as "The Father's Blessing"

From the Beginning, we have continually done our best to acknowledge the Holy Spirit as the main and only star. We have never tried to be a "one-man show" but have always worked with multi-leadership and a variety of speakers, both from our own church and those from many different nations. Honouring the anointing, gifting and calling in others, even from different streams, we are not afraid to learn from them; not afraid of losing our platform even to the point of taking a few risks with controversial individuals. Some we just choose not to ask back.

Always willing to give the Blessing away, there has been a strong release or impartation of the anointing to others who would then take a heart of revival to their own churches and territories. We have almost "given ourselves right out of business" (smile). People don't have to flock to Toronto as much because revival is happening in their own backyards.

How can leaders prepare themselves to receive a fresh move of the Spirit and also nurture it? I offer you some suggestions in Chapter Nine

Chapter Nine

PREPARING TO WELCOME REVIVAL

I think you would agree that in these days, the Lord is catching the attention of His church in unprecedented ways, shaking us, challenging us, and transforming us. He is knocking us out of our man-made religious traditions and safe boxes, shaping us to be radical people of His Kingdom!

When the Holy Spirit's power comes, He shakes us out of religious apathy, lethargy, and indifference, into ZELOS: Rom 12:11, AMP. *"Be aglow & burning with the spirit."* Zelos means fervent, zealous, fiery hot, with living fervour. That sounds like something quite opposite from dignified, cold, and unemotional; behaviours which are often equated with proper, reverent, church practices. In a Christian context, this verse signifies a high spiritual temperature inflamed by the Holy Spirit.

I have no idea how you are going to embrace the Lord's revival when He pours out upon you individually or corporately. However, I'd like to leave you some suggestions as to how you might prepare yourself to receive and also to nurture His fresh move in your midst.

Go to "watering holes" where revival is taking place.

Where in North America are things happening right now? Often the move is transferrable. How open, interested or desperate are you? I have heard several sad comments by pastors such as, "I can't be bothered", "Why not just wait here? If God wants us to have it He'll bring it here!"

One actually said, when I was speaking in his church, "Listen! If God orders the pizza He can deliver it and pay for it, too!" By that he meant a revival move or outpouring of the Spirit. What a dreadful, disrespectful attitude.

Think of the woman who had hemorrhaging for twelve years. Her story is told in Matthew 8:20-22; Mark 5:25-34 and Luke 8:43-48. Yes, she believed that if she could just touch the hem of Jesus' garment she would be healed. She did and she was! I wonder what the outcome would have been if she had just sat at home and said, "Well, I sure believe that Jesus can heal me so I'll just wait here until He comes to my house." No, she had to go to where the Anointing was. I'm sure it was quite a struggle and sacrifice for her to do this.

It's not fully understood why, but history shows that God uniquely uses a specific place or location, and by going there, people receive an impartation to take back to their homes, churches, towns, and nations.

Read all you can about past revivals

Find out all you can from the abundance of great literature published as a result of outpourings of the Spirit. Also watch DVDs of various Toronto meetings. These will help you not only be hungrier but more comfortable with it.

Receive by faith

Be willing to take risks; be persistent; come as a child and press in taking what God offers. Avoid the "uh uh - must keep up the pastoral image you know! What might others think?"

Soak in the Spirit

This has actually been one of the most vital aspects of the Toronto Blessing – right from the beginning. It should probably have been number one on this list.

Soaking is simply coming to be with Father God without agendas or prayer lists – just being still in His Presence without striving, choosing to rest, and longing to experience Him. Don't get concerned about the term "experience". So many critics have said, "that's all those people are looking for - experience, experience, experience." However, Paul wrote of experience in Ephesians 3: 16-19. Note that in Paul's opinion, experiencing God's love far surpasses simply having knowledge about Him, but without experience. There is a deep need for each one of us to be close to God. Experiencing Him is something to be sought after, not avoided.

There have been some very down-to-earth descriptions for the practice of soaking. Some compare it to being like a sponge, which immersed in water, becomes surrounded, saturated and filled to point of the water being able to be squeezed out. Soaking in the Lord's presence can so fill us that His life will pour out of us as we move through our day, touching our families, our workplace, and our church.

Carol Arnott has used the example of a cucumber becoming a pickle. Once a pickle is marinated, i.e. soaked in brine and pickling solution for several weeks, it no longer tastes like a cucumber, it has taken on the flavour of the solution. Think about being so marinated in the presence of the Holy Spirit, soaking in the River of God, and discovering that your old "taste" is gone and you have taken on the flavour of the Holy Spirit.

I like to compare it to marinating a tough, old steak until it becomes tenderized and edible. Believe me, I have witnessed many tough, unbending, inflexible believers become ones who flow in grace and new passion for their Lord as their lives have been changed through this practice of soaking.

When we soak we focus on Him. This puts us in the position where we are often more able to hear His voice and receive His love. It is also an opportunity to pour out our hearts to Him. It's about living in and enjoying an on-going relationship with our Creator. One could say that it's the ultimate heart-to-heart love affair. It's the development of a wonderful friendship.

Simple devotions won't do this; not inter-cessions, not reading. There is a need to be in a quiet place to come to know His heart; a place with no reservations, with our walls down. While we base our theology on the Bible, our experiences with God make the truth come alive and we literally begin to experience the reality of those things we believe.

Friendship is the key to intimacy. He has lots of servants and lots of children but how many deep friends does He have? A prophetic word came forth a couple of years ago which said, "Over 90% of my children live out of concepts about God but few know my heart."

Soaking is a place of vulnerability; to lie down or get comfortable in His Presence with words like, "Father, pour down your love and nurture me this day" or "Lord, I invite you to come close to me." Your love songs to the Lord will cease being rote and will flow from your heart.

I encourage you to make this a priority in your own life. It will soften and transform your soul; you will become so much more aware of the Lord's presence, His voice, and His heart.

There's no need to be legalistic about when and how much you do it but more is better. I believe the Lord longs for intimate, one-on-one times with each of us and because of the responsibilities of life, special times with Him usually are at the end of the day's list and frequently missed altogether.

As a pastor, when soaking becomes a priority for you, let your congregation see that it is such, even giving opportunity to them to do it corporately with quiet worship. Wow, soaking on a Sunday morning rather than preaching could really change a service!! The Holy Spirit will surely know He is welcome in your midst and know He is more than just a heavenly errand boy or mascot.

Many have small groups gather together in their homes to foster this time with the Lord. What an opportunity to grow together!

We have Soaking Schools all over the world now and hearts are being dramatically changed.

Be adventurous

Be daring enough to invite a speaker to your church who has been impacted by revival. Often they're anointed to impart revival to you. However, you don't just want a temporary flash! You want to be able to sustain it. A visitation is one thing but we look to build a habitation for the Lord where He knows He is always welcome.

Receive as much as you can

Desire to receive from the Lord when, where, and as often as you can. Frequently, a pastor's attitude is: "I'm OK. Thank you"; "I'm just fine, I don't need anything else!" or "I've too much to do to take the time necessary." Sometimes leaders can be somewhat independent, often finding it hard to receive.

This could be the result of being driven to perform all the time. We see more and more leaders changing their attitudes about this to, "Yes, yes, here I am, Lord, whatever you have for me!"

Receive prayer and impartation whenever possible from those who carry a revival anointing. It is highly transferable.

Bring "renewal" with you wherever you go.

Take your heart and "flavour" of revival into whatever ministry group you attend. Boast on Him, on His goodness, on His outpouring. We don't have to be ashamed of the Holy Spirit, neither do we have to stand up for Him. Be a person who is known to love the River of God.

Create an environment

In your services create or allow an environment that welcomes the Holy Spirit. Have tender intimate worship to God, especially exalting Jesus, as well as times of praise. There is a considerable difference between exuberant praise and heartfelt worship. I remember that Ruth Heflin, in her book on the Glory, exhorts us to "Praise… until the worship comes. Worship … until the Glory comes. Then … Stand in the Glory!"[3]

Time of personal ministry

Be prepared for ministry to others at the end of each service: such prayer time should include impartation and blessing from a trained and trustworthy team.

---

[3] Ruth Ward Heflin, *Glory, Experiencing the Atmosphere of Heaven* (Hagerstown: The McDougal Publishing Company, 1990) Introduction.

Plan a teaching series

People really need solid, informed, teaching on the person and work of the Holy Spirit. Sometimes I get the impression leaders expect their people to receive by osmosis without offering any solid teaching. It's just taken for granted that people are acquainted with the Spirit and His ways. Teach them about revival history so they can have a broader view of Christianity. If you can't get people out to teaching series, then consider presenting these truths in a sermon series.

Make sure renewal/revival is one of your values.

As a church or ministry, value the work of the Holy Spirit as part of your identity, not just a side issue for a month-long program. Developing a Holy Spirit mentality yourself will help your people "own" or appreciate that value as well.

No "been there, done that" attitude.

Early in the revival, I travelled to a South African church as a conference speaker. I was quite excited to visit a particular city as I had heard reports that a very large, popular church was experiencing a move of God similar to what was happening in Toronto. My first question upon meeting my host was "What's happening at ....?" and was shocked when the response was, "Oh yeah, well it's shut down. The pastor said, 'been there, done that – now we're moving on to street evangelism'." I literally felt a deep grieving in my spirit and cried out, "Oh Lord, we've hardly been anywhere or done anything yet with You. We're just beginning."

Learning a great lesson during that trip, I came to realize that many places just taste the first stages of revival; an introduction, almost. Staying there and playing like little children, they never get past the shoreline and the shallow waters to enter into greater depths of His River. As adults, who would become bored in the shallows, they assume that's all there is.

In Toronto, we were allowed to be child-like in the shallow waters for a few years, getting rid of a lot of religious starch. However, the Lord would not let us stay there. He led us into new depths of worship. He made us recognize and acknowledge that even as Christians we still needed a lot of cleansing from sinful, hurtful attitudes and behaviours. It became an intense time of sanctification for many. He brought us into an awareness that fruitfulness, in any realm of life, really only comes from intimacy and that the best place to be was when we were totally out of our depth, over our heads in His River, having to trust the Spirit to hold us up and lead us on

Allow time and welcome testimonies.

There's power in testimony! Have people, who have been influenced and changed by Revival experiences, share their stories. Hearing words of first-hand accounts releases faith.

Find out what God is doing internationally.

Bring various streams together. Psalm 46:4 says, *"there is a river whose streams make glad the city of God"* (NIV). It's wonderful to have support from others and nowadays we are seeing many churches flow together in the River, moving in unity, yet each bringing their own distinct flavour to the body of Christ. It is sad to see believers remaining isolated and insulated in their own little circles.

Earnestly desire Spiritual Gifts.

Become more knowledgeable and equipped to operate the supernatural abilities of the Holy Spirit. I call them "Spiritual tools for Spiritual tasks." Paul gives a list of them in 1 Corinthians 12: 7-11: word of wisdom, word of knowledge, faith, gifts of healing, working of miracles, prophecy, discerning of spirits, tongues and interpretation of tongues. We need to start using the tools of the Kingdom to do the works of the Kingdom and achieve Kingdom success and fruitfulness. Encourage your people to be flowing in these, too

Step out and start praying for others.

Faith, obedience and persistence pays off. God is definitely catching the attention of His church. He is shaking us, challenging us, and transforming us from

109

a religious institution to His intended family, the body of Christ, sons and daughters who literally reflect His character, His ways and His Glory.

He is causing us to be a revived people catching the wind of the Spirit as He sovereignly blows through His church.

Chapter Ten

WINDS OF CHANGE

When I think of revival, I think of change. Our church family and our individual lives became changed forever after the wind of the Spirit began to blow upon us in 1994. We embarked on the adventure of a life-time! The Lord opened our eyes to see Him in a new way. As well, revival has caused us to see one another in the body of Christ with a different perspective, far beyond denominational boundaries.

We Christians can become quite tunnel-visioned focussing only on our own kind. We can be totally unaware of the awesome and unique things God is doing amongst His people in different places and through different streams. Some of us have a hard time appreciating the diversity in the body of Christ, believing that "our way is the only way!"

Change is uncomfortable. "I like what I like and what I'm used to. I don't care for change!" many say. We all have differences. My husband Bill loved to eat liver – yuk – I like chicken and casseroles. One of my best friends takes her coffee with real cream only – I like mine black, sweet, and sometimes flavoured. I prefer to wear slacks – another friend chooses to wear a skirt. In churches, some rely on hymn books while others use power point displayed on a screen. Some are locked into organ music and choirs while others love guitars, keyboards and drums. Some welcome women into the pulpit, some do not. Some sprinkle with water while others "dunk".

In the revival we came to realize that while we may not agree on forms, structures and programs, when we major on the "majors" we will have the unity that brings forth the commanded blessing of God. Those "majors" are: the fantastic love of our heavenly Father; the saving grace that comes only through Jesus Christ; the closeness, friendship and guidance of the Holy Spirit; and the inerrancy of Scripture. We can have unity in diversity.

The world is looking on, waiting to see unity in the multi-faceted Christian family. Our prayer ministry team has members of practically every denomination and they truly love, honour and respect one another. It's great to witness a Messianic Jew ministering alongside a Charismatic Catholic; a

Fellowship Baptist alongside a Presbyterian; an Anglican alongside a Nazarene.

BECOMING NEW WINESKINS

If we remain stuck in our traditions and preferences, resisting change, we become inflexible and rigid and can be compared to "old wine-skins."

> *"And no one pours new wine into old wineskins. If he does, the wine will burst the skins, the wine will run out and the wineskins will be ruined. No, new wine must be poured into new wineskins."*

Luke 5:3, 38 NIV

These years of revival are ones in which the Holy Spirit has been patiently softening, oiling and molding us; transforming us from old, brittle wineskins into ones which can contain the new wine of His Presence. He is changing us into a people who love Him passionately and who will fruitfully carry His Life and His Kingdom into the world around us.

In this time of transformation, there were months of exuberant, major forging ahead with the Spirit. He vigorously caught our attention! Then He would lead us through more quiet, restful, healing seasons. I often felt saddened when onlookers would declare, "Ha, see, the revival is over. We knew it wouldn't last!" They had no clue as to what was happening in people's hearts during those calmer times.

It seems to take so long to be fashioned into a new wineskin, doesn't it!

Each season is like a new day when the Holy Spirit calls us to walk in new ways. While He never changes, it seems He prods us to change quite regularly so we won't get lukewarm and content in a rut which could become religious.

I recall the evening when He prodded me quite directly. I was at one side of the platform during worship, not really joining in but just quietly standing watching what was happening around me. I sensed the Spirit say to me, "You, know, you treat me just like you do your husband." Somewhat taken aback I replied, "What do you mean?" He said, "You treat me just like an old comfortable, floppy pair of slippers." I got it and began to cry.

While I really loved my husband there was, after many years of marriage, the tendency to be so relaxed together; to almost take one another for granted; to be so comfortable with each other that there were few surprises left any more. The Spirit was saying, in effect, "I don't want you to ever lose the wonder and expectation and joy of being in my Presence – ever!"

The other thing we've come to realize is that no matter what group we align ourselves with, we don't have all the answers and we're not always right. Even the Apostle Paul was challenged in the

Corinthian church because some liked one person's form of ministry over another's and so caused dissention. This problem is addressed in 1 Corinthians, chapter 3.

BECOMING A PEOPLE OF REVIVAL

When the Holy Spirit comes in power He shakes us to our deepest places – to the core of our being. He is causing us to be a "people of revival." What do I mean by that?

First of all, revival is a thing of the Spirit, not of man and we can't make it happen. It's not our choice. We can't control it. We can't make it stop and start at our will as if it were a mechanical tool. Granted, we can let the Holy Spirit know whether He's welcome or not. Revival is not something we decide to, *do because we need a new program for the church this year so we'll have a revival."* Maybe a church really does need a new program but this one won't come from a board meeting.

What does the word revival mean? Some expressions which can be used to describe revival are: to come back to life; to be invigorated; to be renewed or refreshed; to be made new; to be stirred into action; or to be awakened like coming out of a sleep. Remember the story in Chapter Five of the "crowing rooster" calling, "Wake up, wake up, it's a new day!"

Revival is for the church, bringing her to life again; out of dry, dead, fruitless places. Revival is much more than just having big successful churches, exciting conferences, awesome meetings. It's to bring a total change of life – of hearts – which would bring change to families, to communities and eventually to a nation.

Revival is more than just a big bang. Yes, the Holy Spirit came with a big bang in 1994 startling us out of our old patterns but it was unto something. It was to get our attention. Revival brings change! The laughter, the joy, the exuberance broke the old wineskin open. It was to set us up for our assignment in the world. True revival will change our walk. It's a moment by moment walk with the Lord, not just a momentary flash. I once heard the comment, "I don't care how high you fly, how firm is your walk here on earth."

Let me share just some of areas where we are seeing revival happening.

A Revival of Revelation:

The Apostle Paul, in his letter to the Ephesian church, writes that he constantly prays for the believers to receive a spirit of revelation into the mysteries of God by having their hearts flooded with light so they could know and understand the awesome reality of being in Christ and the power of God which dwells within them.

Revelation means a startling disclosure of something you didn't previously know; your eyes and ears are suddenly opened. "Wow", you say! "Now I see it! Now I grasp it!"

In these years there is a breaking out of prophetic people like never before with accurate words from the heart of God to His people. There's an increase of the "seer" anointing where people can discern more quickly and see into the spiritual realm more clearly. There's an increase in manifestations of the nine gifts/abilities of the Spirit that Paul writes about in 1 Corinthians 12. There's an increase in understanding the times and seasons we are in and those which are approaching. There's an increase in the ability to hear the voice of God. Along with such revelation comes a revival of the Word.

A Revival of the Word:

There is a deeper hunger for understanding the scriptures. In 1 Corinthians 2:9, Paul says that no eye has seen, no ear has heard, no mind has conceived what God has prepared for those who love Him (speaking about the natural man) but God has revealed it to us by His Spirit. Eyes are being opened to see and take hold of the promises and principles of the Word. There's a fresh hunger in the church for the life and the spirit of the Bible – not just the letter of the law but the life which is in the Word. May I suggest that you read Psalms 119 from the New Passion Translation by Brian Simmons – Wow!

117

I remember an old adage which is as new as "right now": "If we just have the Word alone, we dry up: if we just have the Spirit alone, we blow up; if we have the Spirit and Word together, we grow up."

Many, many believers, who had become "spiritually anorexic" from not being nourished, are now, after being revived, hungry for the milk and meat of the Word.

A Revival of Expectations:

As they are revived, believers are coming out of passivity and lax attitudes toward walking out their Christian faith. For example, some may say "Well, I'm just waiting on God. If He wants me to have it He'll give it to me sooner or later." I once heard someone say, "For heaven's sake, He's twenty miles down the road waiting on you! Get going!"

I exhort people to remember what God has already said to them – what hopes, what promises, what prophetic encouragements, what potential, what call. We need to come into agreement with what He has said. Embrace it by faith, step out and put action to it, without apology. Then watch Him as He leads your next step. His timing is perfect!

Several years ago I realized what dismal expectations I had regarding the fulfillment of many similar personal prophetic words. They were gathering dust, so to speak, on a shelf waiting for some miraculous "poof" to happen. I liked them, was blessed and thankful for what I heard, but was very passive in my response. Like so many people, I guess I thought that God would just plunk the fulfillment down from the heavens somewhere.

Then one evening, Ruth Ward Heflin spoke a powerful prophetic word over me. A portion of it went like this:

"Greater healing, greater miracles, greater emphasis on the miraculous.

*Greater **expectations** in thine heart. For as the **expectation** comes, the miracles shall happen.*

*As the **expectation** comes, yea, the signs shall come.*

*Oh, according to the **expectation** of thy heart, if you shall **expect** it, it shall be.*

***Expect** the unexpected, ha, ha.*

***Expect** what you've never had in your ministry before.*

***Expect** the fullness of all that I've called thee unto.*

'And know this', sayeth the Lord. 'It is on thee this night. Go not in former ways or in former expectations, nor in former plans, but every time consider it may be your last moment to minister. And minister in the fullness, and minister in the fullness,

119

and minister in the fullness and you shall see the fullness come forth,' sayeth the Lord."

Wow! What a word! Can you see a common emphasis all through it? In spite of such a clear message, I simply entered into the waiting game once again. Ten years later, the Holy Spirit shockingly brought this prophecy to my attention and I was deeply convicted, with many tears, of my lackadaisical attitude toward His exhortation. I now choose to move on with fresh vision and expectations of fulfillment. Let Him revive you in this area, too.

A Revival of Apostolic and Prophetic Leadership:

We are seeing a different form of church government emerging. There is new leadership language being heard. Many revived churches are embracing the Ephesians 4 model where everyone is equipped to do the work of the ministry as they mature in the Lord. Less and less are there just a select few in a hierarchical, empire building structure. Spiritual mothers and fathers are rising up who recognize the gifting in their church families and release their people to do the works of the Kingdom.

A Revival of Desire and Passion:

There is revival in our hearts as we experience a new warmth for the Lord; a longing to experience His love and a passion for Him that goes beyond words. We are being transformed from being simply "mental assent" believers to ones who are coming to know the reality of His Life in our spirits. Imagine really being in love with the Lord. Being "in love" is an all encompassing, moment-by-moment reality as opposed to simply "loving" as a choice. The only comparison I can make may seem pretty earthy. Consider it as a parable.

What was it like when you were first really in love in the natural? The object of your affection was simply everything to you. You felt you couldn't survive another day without hearing that familiar voice, seeing that precious form, feeling that warm hand, and looking onto those wonderful eyes. A day without communication was cold, barren and lonely. I could elaborate more but that should get the point across.

The Holy Spirit is wooing and fashioning us into a company of radical lovers of God, as He transforms and revives our hearts.

A Revival of His Presence:

This is probably one of the most significant aspects of the revival today. One could actually call it a Presence Revival. He has promised that He will always be with us. Much of the time, we have accepted that fact simply by faith because the Word says so. Of course, that faith acceptance should never change throughout our life. However, there are now, in the midst of revival, times of an actual physical, acute awareness of His Presence.

We have tasted, felt and seen the tangible manifest presence of His Glory and once having tasted this, we long for more. There are times when you feel you can almost touch Him, feel His breath and the weightiness of His Presence. He is real, not just a theological theory!

His Presence changes everything! It not only captivates and transforms individuals, but if welcomed, He will change our churches and our programs as we choose to walk in lock-step with Him.

In Exodus 33, we read how Moses would go a distance away from the tribes of people to a tent in order to have personal time with the Lord. God would meet with him in manifested Presence and speak with him face to face as with a friend. Moses went beyond familiar territory in order to seek God, to meet with Him. Desperate to know that the Lord would lead the Children of Israel to their promised land, he asked the Lord to give him the principles, rules, and ways to do this. God simply replied with the promise, "My Presence will go with you." In other words, "That's all you'll need Moses, My Presence." God gives us the same promise today, "My Presence goes with you."

That's all we need – His Presence! Hunger for it, long for it, expect it! Desperation for God is one of the keys to revival and He does not disappoint.

Well, dear readers, this has not been the whole story, but is enough for now. I trust that it has given you a glimpse of the joys and challenges we faced as we chose to welcome the Spirit into our church and our lives.

"Once Upon a Revival..." is His-story. It is history in the making and continues as Father, Jesus, and the Holy Spirit are never finished with us. It is a never ending chronicle of love, restoration, and wonder.

We continue to move on...

ABOUT THE AUTHOR

Mary Audrey has been on the Catch the Fire pastoral team since 1993. With her exhorting, mentoring and teaching skills she has ministered to both men and women in large and small groups, seminars, retreats, and conferences both in the local church and internationally.

A few of her favorite topics are The Gifts of The Spirit; Finding Your Place in the Body of Christ; God's Heart and Plan for Women; the Mystery and Challenges of Marriage; and Developing a Revival Culture, along with other themes designed to bring believers into walking in the Spirit with wholeness and fruitfulness.

Ministering in a wide variety of churches for over 30 years, both locally and internationally, her heart is for unity in the body of Christ.

She is the founder of Releasers of Life, a cross-denominational ministry called to awaken, equip and release women and men into their potential and destiny through conferences, retreats and seminars. She has written a number of teaching manuals and her book, *Releasers of Life: Discover the River Within,* has been translated into several languages.

Inquiries about Mary Audrey's teaching materials may be directed to rayleasers@sympatico.ca

Her books, *Releasers of Life, Discover the River Within* and *Once Upon a Revival* **may be ordered from: Amazon.com Shekinahchurch.org (734) 662-6040 resource.catchthefire.com**

22912004R00069

Made in the USA
Charleston, SC
06 October 2013